HOT

Celebrity Biographies

Miley Cyrus

MUSIC AND TV SUPERSTAR

SHEILA ANDERSON

Enslow Publishers, Inc.
40 Industrial Road
Box 398
Berkeley Heights, NJ 07922
USA
http://www.enslow.com

Library of Congress Cataloging-in-Publication Data
Anderson, Sheila.
  Miley Cyrus : music and TV superstar / Sheila Anderson.
    p. cm. — (Hot celebrity biographies)
  Includes bibliographical references and index.
  Summary: "Find out how Miley Cyrus became Hannah Montana, her hobbies, awards, and likes and dislikes"—Provided by publisher.
  ISBN-13: 978-0-7660-3213-2
  ISBN-10: 0-7660-3213-2
  1. Cyrus, Miley, 1992—Juvenile literature. 2. Singers—United States—Biography—Juvenile literature. 3. Television actors and actresses—United States—Biography—Juvenile literature. I. Title.
  ML3930.C98A53 2009
  782.42164092—dc22
  [B]
                              2008026462

Paperback ISBN-13: 978-0-7660-3213-2
Paperback ISBN-10: 0-7660-3628-4

Printed in the United States of America

10 9 8 7 6 5 4 3 2 1

To our readers: We have done our best to make sure all Internet Addresses in this book were active and appropriate when we went to press. However, the author and the publisher have no control over and assume no liability for the material available on those Internet sites or on other Web sites they may link to. Any comments or suggestions can be sent by e-mail to comments@enslow.com or to the address on the back cover.

♻ Enslow Publishers, Inc., is committed to printing our books on recycled paper. The paper in every book contains 10% to 30% post-consumer waste (PCW). The cover board on the outside of each book contains 100% PCW. Our goal is to do our part to help young people and the environment too!

Photographs: Damian Dovarganes/AP Images, 1; Matt Sayles/AP Images, 4, 19, 33, 43; John Hayes/AP Images, 7; Evan Agostini/AP Images, 8; Jennifer Graylock/AP Images, 9; Amanda Parks/AP Images, 11; Frank Gunn/The Canadian Press/AP Images, 13; Jason DeCrow/AP Images, 14; Kevork Djansezian/AP Images, 17, 20, 39; Mary Altaffer/AP Images, 22; Jennifer Graylock/AP Images, 23; Amanda Parks/AP Images, 25; Chris Polk/AP Images, 27; Tammie Arroyo/AP Images, 28; Jeff Christensen/AP Images, 31; Gus Ruelas/AP Images, 34; Chris Pizzello/AP Images, 36; Matt Sayles/AP Images for Fox, 41

Cover photo: Miley Cyrus appears onstage during MTV's *Total Request Live* in 2006. Damian Dovarganes/AP Images.

Contents

Who Is Miley Cyrus?

Just about everybody has heard the name of pop star and Disney sensation Miley Ray Cyrus. But did you know her name hasn't always been Miley? Well, it's true! Yes, the television character Hannah Montana is played by Miley Cyrus. But this popular young star's parents didn't call her Miley Ray when she was born. They named her Destiny Hope Cyrus. They gave her this name because they thought that one day she would accomplish great things. Boy, were they right. The name "Miley" came later.

Destiny Hope Cyrus was a happy girl from the time she was a baby. She always had a smile on her face. Her dad adored his little girl. Because of her cheerful personality and constant smile, he began calling her "Smiley." Soon the nickname got shortened to "Miley," and it stuck. By the time she started school, that's what everyone called her. But it wasn't until January 2008 that the talented actor and musician started the process to legally change her name from Destiny Hope Cyrus to Miley Ray Cyrus.

◀ *Miley Cyrus arrives at the VH1 Awards in 2006. Cyrus has two sides: sparkling superstar and ordinary kid.*

WHAT'S IN A NAME?

Destiny Hope Cyrus earned the nickname Miley when she was young because she was so smiley. Then she later changed her name legally. Here are some other interesting bits of trivia about the young star's name:

• Miley Cyrus's grandmother is the one person who still calls her by her birth name, Destiny.

• Jason Earles is Miley and Billy Ray Cyrus's costar on *Hannah Montana.* He feels so close to them that he jokingly calls himself Jason Ray Cyrus.

• Miley took the middle name Ray in 2008 to honor her dad, Billy Ray Cyrus.

Miley Cyrus was born on November 23, 1992. She grew up in a small Tennessee town called Franklin. Franklin is close to Nashville, Tennessee, which is known as the country music capital of the world.

Miley and her family lived on a farm. They owned lots of animals, including dogs, cats, chickens, fish, horses, and cows. Miley was a regular country girl. Her family briefly lived in Toronto, Canada, while Miley's dad worked on a television series there. But for most of her life, Miley called Tennessee home.

That is, until a big opportunity brought the Cyrus family to Los Angeles, California, in December 2005. Miley and her

▲ *Miley Cyrus performs with her dad, Billy Ray Cyrus, in 2006.*

dad both were cast on the Disney television series *Hannah Montana*, and the family moved to California to be closer to their work. The Cyruses still have their farm in Tennessee. They go back to Tennessee when they can, but most of the time you'll find them in sunny California.

Miley comes from a large blended family. Her father is actor and country singer Billy Ray Cyrus. (Have you ever heard the song "Achy Breaky Heart"? That was his big hit back in 1992.) Miley's mother is Leticia Cyrus, who goes by the nickname "Tish." Miley has five siblings. Some of them are half-siblings who were born to each of her parents before

▲ *Her mother, Tish, (right) is one of Miley Cyrus's biggest role models.*

they met. Her half-siblings include an older sister, Brandi, and two older brothers, Christopher Cody and Trace. She also has a younger brother, Braison Chance, and a younger sister, Noah Lindsey.

Her sister Brandi is a musician just like Miley and her dad. Sometimes Brandi even plays guitar for Miley when she performs live. Miley's brother Trace also is a musician. He sings and plays guitar for a rock band in California. Her little sister, Noah, is an aspiring actress. She has made several appearances on *Hannah Montana*. It's obvious that performing is definitely in the Cyrus family!

TWO SIDES TO MILEY

Miley has an outgoing, bubbly personality. If you've seen *Hannah Montana*, you know she's got a sense of humor!

Her positive energy and enthusiasm are what got her the role of Hannah Montana.

Miley has always been a performer. "Watch me," she was always telling the people around her when she was little. "I've always loved singing, and I've always loved acting and dancing," she says.

Miley admits that she loves being in the spotlight. "What I like most is the crowd interaction," she has said. "That's really cool." She gets a kick out of being recognized by fans on the street. She is thrilled when she's onstage and sees her fans singing her songs along with her. "There's nothing more fun than being onstage and getting the vibe from the crowd," she says. "There's nothing like being on a set where you are there to make other people happy and to make them laugh. That's the best job in the world."

But Miley's life is not all sparkles. She has a pretty normal life at home.

▶ *Miley Cyrus promotes* Hannah Montana *at a media event in 2006.*

Her parents expect her to do chores like any ordinary kid. One of her jobs is to load the dishwasher. Just like other kids her age, Miley does homework too. And she sometimes fights with her brothers and her little sister. When she does get in trouble, Miley's parents ground her. And even though she earns money acting and singing, Miley is not allowed to spend all her earnings. Her parents give her part of what she makes as an allowance. Most of her income goes into an investment fund for when she is older.

Miley also relies on her Christian faith to guide her. She goes to church with her family every Sunday. She always takes her Bible with her when she travels. "My mom gives me cool little Bibles, or she'll print out verses and make scrapbooks for me," she says.

While Miley is an ordinary kid in many ways, she doesn't go to school every day like most kids. Before she got her role on *Hannah Montana*, Miley attended Heritage Middle School in Tennessee. But since she started to act, she spends most days rehearsing and filming the show. So instead of going to a regular school, Miley studies with a private tutor three hours each day. "I do three hours of school in the morning, whether I'm on set, whether I'm on tour," she explained. "You get it done before you start your day."

▲ *Miley's real-life dad, Billy Ray Cyrus, plays her character's dad in* Hannah Montana.

Miley studies hard. Actually, she plans to graduate from high school early! She is taking college prep courses so that she'll be ready if she decides to go to college.

What's a typical day for Miley? She arrives at rehearsal in the morning, sometimes still in her pajamas. When she's not working, she meets with her private tutor.

Part of Miley's routine includes spending a couple of hours getting her hair and makeup done. In between practicing her lines for *Hannah Montana*, she does interviews and poses for photo shoots.

11

PERSONAL STATS

Original name: Destiny Hope Cyrus

Birthday: November 23, 1992

Parents: Leticia and Billy Ray Cyrus

Siblings: Two older half-brothers Christopher Cody and Trace, older half-sister Brandi, and younger brother Braison Chance and sister Noah Lindsey

MILEY'S FRIENDS

Miley still misses her friends back home in Tennessee, including her best friend, Tory Sparkman. But she has made new friends since moving to Los Angeles. Some of her closest friends are her *Hannah Montana* costars Mitchel Musso and Emily Osment. Miley says that Emily is her best friend in Los Angeles. The two have even shared their hobbies with each other. Miley taught Emily how to play guitar, and Emily taught Miley how to knit.

Miley has had opportunities to meet and become friends with other Disney actors as well. She considers Ashley Tisdale and Vanessa Hudgens from *High School Musical* good friends. Miley and her friends like to hang out and have sleepovers just like ordinary teenagers.

Miley also considers her mom, Tish, one of her closest friends. She relates well to both of her parents. Miley says her parents are "just the coolest and the chillest."

What Miley Likes

So many people love Miley Cyrus on *Hannah Montana*. What's not to love? She's funny, and she gets caught up in some interesting situations. The character Miley Stewart does her best to live an ordinary life when she's not performing on

▲ *Miley Cyrus speaks in an interview with* The Canadian Press *in 2007.*

▲ *Miley Cyrus appears onstage during MTV's* Total Request Live *in 2006.*

stage as Hannah Montana. She goes to the beach and to the movies with her best friends, Lilly and Oliver. She deals with her annoying brother at home. So what is the real Miley— Miley Cyrus—like? Well, she's actually not much different.

Considering she was raised on a farm, it should be no surprise that Cyrus loves animals. She grew up surrounded by them. Back in Tennessee, Cyrus used to enjoy braiding the horses' tails. She learned how to ride a horse when she was just a toddler. Horseback riding is still a hobby she enjoys when she gets back to the farm.

Cyrus and her family also have a number of dogs that live on the Nashville farm and at her other home in Los Angeles.

Cyrus's love for animals goes even further than keeping them as pets. She cares about how animals are treated. Cyrus does not agree with the way that animals raised for food are treated, so she chooses not to eat meat. She is a vegetarian.

Another of Cyrus's passions is music. When she has down time, Cyrus often can be found writing songs or playing her guitar. About songwriting she says, "When you write or sing a song that means something to you, you are saying, 'You know what? This is who I am!'" Cyrus wrote the song "I Miss You," which appears on her second album, for her grandfather after he passed away.

Cyrus likes listening to pop and rock music. Her musical idols are Hilary Duff, Kelly Clarkson, Ashlee Simpson, and country superstar Shania Twain. Clarkson's *Breakaway* is one of Cyrus's favorite albums. Other musicians she likes are Mariah Carey, Justin Timberlake, and the band The Killers. She says she loves the band's *Hot Fuss* album.

ROLE MODELS

Cyrus says she looks up to Duff because she acts like herself and isn't fake. She respects Duff because Duff has not let fame go to her head. "Hilary Duff has been my role model forever," Cyrus has said. "She's a normal girl."

MILEY'S FAVORITES

Color: Pink

Song: "Achy Breaky Heart" (Sung by her dad, Billy Ray Cyrus!)

TV shows: *The Suite Life of Zach & Cody, Laguna Beach*

Sport: Cheerleading

Singers: Hilary Duff, Kelly Clarkson, Mariah Carey, Ashlee Simpson

Movie: *Steel Magnolias*

Cyrus likes Twain because she seems to have a lot of fun performing, and she takes risks with her music. Some people compare Cyrus to Twain because they both have an exciting stage presence. They both know how to stir up a crowd, that's for sure!

On a personal level, Cyrus looks up to her mom, Tish, and her big sister, Brandi. She is very close to her family members and considers them to be her role models. "My mom taught me that the most important thing is staying true to yourself," Cyrus explained. As for her dad, she appreciates being able to tell him anything. In fact, it was her dad who inspired Cyrus to go into acting and singing. Her first performance was when she was just a little girl. She joined her dad on stage during one of his musical performances. The two sang the song "Hound Dog."

HER FAVORITE THINGS

Cyrus uses her allowance from acting and singing to pay for one of her favorite hobbies—shopping. "I definitely love to shop!" she says. "Every day after work, my mom and I go shopping."

Cyrus especially likes buying clothes and shoes. "I'm a big shoe person," she says. As if the shopping sprees with her mother aren't enough, she says she shops even more when

▲ *Cyrus arrives at the 2008 Academy Awards with her mom* (right).

she's with her friends. If she can't get to a store or a mall, Cyrus shops online. She says she is happy to buy shoes from discount stores. If she thinks something is cute, she'll buy it. It doesn't have to be the most expensive brand.

Another one of Cyrus's loves is cheerleading. Before she moved to California, she performed on her school's cheerleading team back in Tennessee. She also competed with a cheerleading group called the Premier Tennessee Allstars. She says that cheerleading is her favorite sport. Cyrus also enjoys bike rides, swimming, and hanging out by the pool.

Cyrus's favorite color is pink. "Pink is not just a color. It's an attitude," she says. She often wears pink clothes but likes to mix up bright colors and dark colors. When asked what color crayon she would be, Cyrus answered, "Tickle me pink."

The young star likes to change her style to fit her mood or the occasion. "My style is kind of whatever I feel like wearing," she said. "Sometimes I'll be punky. The next day I'll be preppy."

Cyrus loves to snack. Her favorite snacks are cashews, gummy bears, and peach rings. "I have candy all the time," she says. "I live on gummy bears and peach rings."

▲ Miley Cyrus wore this sequined dress for the People's Choice Awards in 2007. She enjoys changing her look depending on her mood.

Becoming "Hannah Montana"

Hannah Montana has become a huge hit for Disney in recent years. So how did this whole thing get started?

"I auditioned forever," Cyrus recalled. "At first they said I was too small and too young." Cyrus first auditioned for a role on *Hannah Montana* when she was eleven years old. She read for the role of Lilly Truscott—the best friend character on the show—as well as for the lead.

Believe it or not, she didn't get either part! The people that Cyrus auditioned for at Disney worried about her limited acting experience. They didn't know if she had what it took to play a lead character.

Disney continued looking for the right girl for the lead role. After six months, they called Cyrus back to audition again. Now she was twelve years old. Cyrus had to go through one audition after another. Her dad encouraged her during the auditions by saying, "Just be yourself. Go in there and be Miley."

◀ *It took Miley Cyrus six months to win the part of "Hannah Montana."*

▲ *Miley Cyrus promotes Hannah Montana gear.*

It was not a quick process. But it was worth the time she put into it. Before she knew it, the role of Hannah Montana was hers. Gary Marsh, president of Disney Channel Entertainment, said, "She stood in front of us and knocked us out." Her bubbly personality and can-do attitude got her the role that made her a star.

A FAMILY PROJECT

Once she got the role of Hannah Montana, Cyrus had the unusual experience of participating in her dad's audition. He was auditioning for the role of her dad on the show. Of course, he landed the part. So now Cyrus's real dad is also her television dad. Cyrus doesn't mind working with her dad. The two are very close. They try to keep their work life and home life separate.

"What's good is that once my dad and I are home, we are done. We don't even run lines together," she has said.

"Anything that happens on the set stays on the set. . . . We forget that we even work together and just hang out."

Cyrus and her costars have loads of fun hanging out on the set of *Hannah Montana*. She says it's just like being with friends at school. "We just goof off," she says.

Cyrus learns a lot from her dad on the set too. One thing Billy Ray Cyrus has always told his daughter about her work as an actor is that it needs to be fun. "Always have fun with what you're doing," he advises Cyrus. "Don't do it for fame or money. Do it because it's something that you feel is right."

ALL ABOUT *HANNAH MONTANA*

If you're not familiar with *Hannah Montana*, here is the scoop. The main character is Miley Stewart. She lives with

▶ *Cyrus, in character as "Hannah Montana," waits to sign autographs.*

MEET THE CAST OF HANNAH MONTANA

Miley Cyrus has become great friends with the other cast members while working on *Hannah Montana*. Here's a quick run-down of some of the characters they play:

Robbie Stewart: Miley Stewart's dad, played by Billy Ray Cyrus, gave up his own career to raise his kids after his wife died. As Hannah Montana's manager, he always has some useful advice for his daughter.

Lilly Truscot: Miley's best friend, played by Emily Osment, has her own secret identity so that she can hang out with her friend when she's in character as Hannah Montana.

Jackson Stewart: Played by Jason Earles, Miley Stewart's brother provides many of the laughs in *Hannah Montana*. But he's a good brother who helps keep his sister's secret.

Oliver Oken: Another good friend of Miley Stewart, Oliver was in love with Hannah Montana before he realized who she was. He is played by Mitchel Musso.

her dad, Robbie, and her older brother, Jackson, in Los Angeles. Miley Stewart's mother has passed away, so her dad is raising his two kids by himself. Miley Stewart's brother loves to compete with their dad. Their competitions always end up with lots of laughter.

Miley Stewart has her own issues. While she is a rock star by night, she wants to be just a regular kid during the day. That is why she uses a stage name, Hannah Montana, and wears a wig when she performs. By disguising herself as Hannah onstage, the character can lead a normal life the rest of the time.

One of the biggest challenges Miley Stewart faces is keeping her secret identity a secret. She doesn't want the kids at school to know that she is Hannah Montana. She wants her friends to like her for who she really is, not just because she's famous. And she does not want to be bothered by fans wherever she goes like many celebrities are. Her secret is almost revealed several times, but she manages to keep her second identity from being discovered.

Only Miley Stewart's closest friends know that she is Hannah Montana. She has sworn them to secrecy. Her best friend, Lilly, manages to stay by her side when Miley is in Hannah Montana mode. She does this by disguising herself, too,

▼ *The cast of* Hannah Montana *includes* (from left) *Mitchel Musso, Billy Ray Cyrus, Miley Cyrus, Emily Osment, and Jason Earles.*

when she is with Hannah in public. Lilly's secret identity is Lola. Lola wears brightly colored wigs, which is very different from Lilly's style.

Fans love *Hannah Montana*. They think the show is hilarious, and they like the concept of a main character who switches back and forth between being a rock star and a normal girl. Not only that, but each episode teaches a moral, or a lesson. Sometimes the lesson is about honesty. Other times it's about competition or loving yourself for who you are. No matter what the message, the show always has a happy ending—something that both fans and their parents can appreciate. The *Hannah Montana* TV series has been such a success that they made it into a movie too! The movie was filmed in 2008.

Hannah Montana has attracted fans of all ages—from children to adults. Cyrus isn't surprised the show appeals to such a wide range of people. "No matter how old you are, no matter where you come from, you always have a dream or goal that you'd like to achieve," she has said. "It shows just a normal girl reaching her dream. So I think that gives a little bit of inspiration to all the viewers."

HANNAH MONTANA FUN FACTS

• The main character of *Hannah Montana* was originally named Zoe. Then she was called Chloe. When Miley Cyrus got the role, producers decided to use her real first name as the character's name.

• Three of main character Miley Stewart's famous phrases are, "Sweet niblets!", "Say what?!", and "Ya think?!"

• Miley Cyrus's real-life godmother is country singer and actress Dolly Parton, who also plays her godmother on *Hannah Montana.*

• *Hannah Montana* is set in Malibu, California. The Stewarts' house is the same set used for the old TV show *Diagnosis Murder.*

• Every episode is named after a famous song. You'll also hear other musical references if you pay close attention, such as when Robbie Stewart hurts his back and says "Ow, my achy, breaky back!" What popular country song does that remind you of?

▶ Hannah Montana *has won over fans of all ages.*

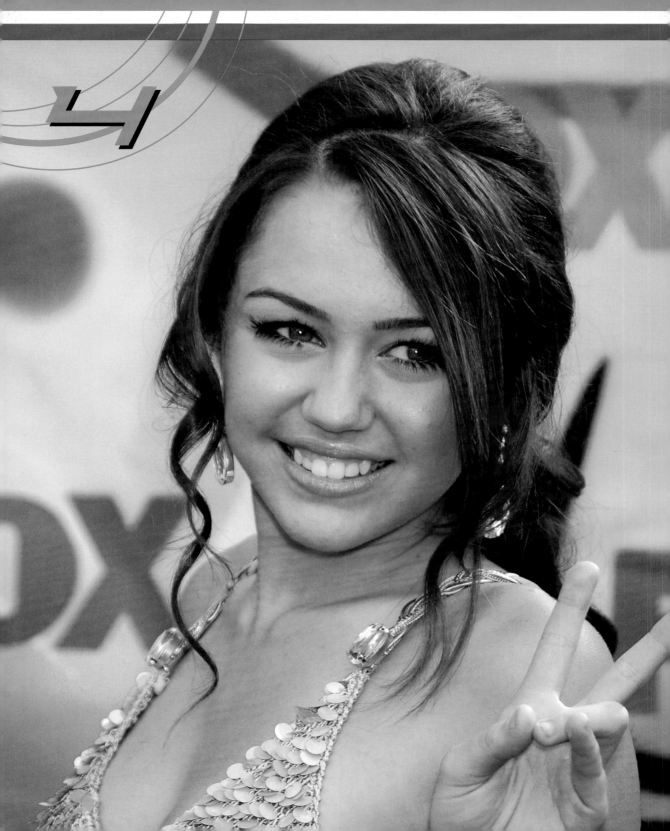

Miley's Career Takes Off

Cyrus first broke into acting when she was nine years old. That was the year she got her first small role. At the time, her dad was working on a television series called *Doc*. He played the show's main character. Cyrus played a guest role on the show. She played the character Kylie on one episode. The same year she got a small part in the movie *Big Fish*. She played young Ruthie. After getting this little taste of acting, Cyrus knew she wanted to be an actress.

In addition to her major role on *Hannah Montana* and these other small parts, Cyrus has had other acting roles. She can be seen in Rhonda Vincent's country music video, "If Heartaches Had Wings." Cyrus appeared as "Hannah Montana" on *The Suite Life of Zach and Cody*. She also was a voice actor on *The Emperor's New School*.

Her acting career has led to other opportunities. She appeared as herself on The Disney Channel Games and Disney Channel's New Year Bowlathon. Cyrus also appeared

◀ *At a young age, Cyrus has become one of the hottest stars around. She is pictured at the Teen Choice Awards in 2007.*

FOLLOWING IN HER FATHER'S FOOTSTEPS

As a successful singer himself, Billy Ray Cyrus couldn't be happier to have such a talented daughter. It was clear to him from the time Miley was a young child that she would someday be a star. "Since she was little, she would look at me confidently and say, 'I'm going to blow by you, Daddy. I'm going to be a singer, songwriter, entertainer,'" the proud father said in an interview with *USA Today*.

Billy Ray Cyrus compares his daughter's talent to Lucille Ball and to late jazz singer Eva Cassidy. "She was born to sing," he told *USA Today*. "Musically, she is—this is the only time I'm going to brag—she's the real deal musically. I can't wait for you to hear what she's been writing and the songs that come from inside of her. You know the saying she's got an old soul? Well, she's got an old soul, and her old soul's got a lot of soul."

in the Macy's Thanksgiving Day Parade and the Walt Disney World Christmas Day Parade.

POP STAR SENSATION

Music has always been a part of Cyrus's life, and performing is a treat for this talented young star. "As soon as I step on that stage, nothing matters," she explains. "I don't think of it as work. It's just so much fun." She enjoys being able to perform as herself and as Hannah Montana on her concert tour. It's fun dressing up, but Cyrus says that the blond wig she wears as part of the costume can be uncomfortable. "It's itchy, really itchy and hot."

Cyrus's songs have positive messages and a fun beat. Songs such as "Who Said" send the message to kids that they can be whatever they want to be; the sky is the limit. Through her music, Cyrus encourages kids to follow their dreams. After all, she followed her dreams and look where they took her! It's important to Cyrus to be a role model to kids. And performing songs with positive lyrics is one way she can do so.

Cyrus has had unbelievable success as a musician. In 2006, she opened for the Cheetah Girls on their North American tour. The following year she was the headlining act with her *Miley Cyrus/Hannah Montana Best of Both Worlds* tour. Fans went wild! Her concerts were so popular that many of them sold out within minutes of tickets becoming available. Some people sold their tickets to fans for thousands of dollars.

For fans who were not able to get tickets to a live concert, it was filmed and released in theaters

▶ *Cyrus performs as "Hannah Montana" on* Good Morning America *in 2007.*

HOT TICKET

Miley Cyrus's 2007–2008 *Best of Both Worlds* tour created a bit of a controversy when tickets for many shows sold out in five minutes or less. Then some tickets were sold on Internet sites such as eBay for much more than their original prices. Some tickets sold for as high as $1,000!

Many fans were disappointed not to be able to see their favorite star in concert when their families couldn't afford the tickets. Cyrus ended up adding fourteen new shows to the tour to give more people a chance to see her perform live. Others could catch the 3-D movie version in theaters.

as a 3-D movie titled *Hannah Montana & Miley Cyrus: Best of Both Worlds Concert.* Miley attended the movie's premiere in Hollywood. "It's the craziest thing to be at your own premiere," she said.

While Cyrus has a blast performing for her fans, she has to work hard to prepare for her concerts. "When preparing for a concert, I do lots of training," she explains. "I work with a choreographer to create moves, and then I have to keep my voice strong with [singing] lessons."

When she's not on the set of *Hannah Montana* or on the road performing, Cyrus often can be found making guest appearances on television programs. She has performed duets with her dad on the *Country Colgate Showdown* and on *Dancing With the Stars.* She also has been a presenter at the American Music Awards, the Annual Country Music Association Awards, and the Teen Choice Awards.

Cyrus's love for music has definitely paid off. She has recorded three albums. The first one is titled *Hannah Montana*. It is a soundtrack for the TV show. The second one is a double disc titled *Hannah Montana 2: Meet Miley Cyrus*. It features songs from the show, as well as Cyrus as herself. Her first two CDs together sold six million copies in two years. Both albums debuted at the top of the Billboard Hot 200 chart. In 2008, Cyrus released her first solo album, *Breakout*.

▼ *Miley Cyrus sings during the 2008 Kids Choice Awards. Her music tends to be upbeat and fun.*

Fame, Fans, and Fashion

Cyrus says that it's fun to be noticed when she's out in public. She loves the attention she gets from fans. But she will admit that sometimes it is difficult to do everyday things. Strangers come up to her all the time—when she's out for a bike ride with friends or eating out with her family.

Sometimes fans will notice her at inconvenient moments. Once at an amusement park, Cyrus was feeling sick after a ride. She remembered that fans who recognized her "were like, 'Hannah Montana is about to puke!'"

But Cyrus understands that attention comes with fame. "I'll be out with my friends and be recognized, and little girls will ask me for my autograph," she said. And Cyrus is thankful for her fans. "It's cool to know people support you," she said. Cyrus gets really pumped up when she sees her fans excited about her music and her acting. Her young fans are so enthusiastic that she even receives invitations to girls' birthday parties all the time.

◀ *Miley Cyrus is known for the energy and enthusiasm she displays onstage, as well as for her fashion sense.*

Whenever she can, Cyrus makes an effort to reach out to fans. While on tour in Las Vegas in early 2008, she took time out of her busy schedule to visit fans at Sunrise Children's Hospital. She posed for photos and signed autographs for sick children there.

While Cyrus likes being noticed, she also enjoys being a role model. It is important to her to set a good example for her fans. She tries to stress "being a good role model and setting high standards for yourself," she has said. She even thinks about the example she is setting when she chooses how to dress.

When she appeared on *Oprah* in 2007, Cyrus explained to Oprah Winfrey why she cares. "I like to look kind of like what girls would want to look up to, and their moms and dads will say, 'Hey, that's cool. That's different.'"

It's important to Cyrus that her fans' parents will approve of the example she's setting. "I've got to make really good decisions," she says. "And that helps me in my real life because it's that little voice in my head telling me right from wrong. More than just for myself, but for the girls who are watching me."

AWARDS AND RECOGNITION

"Hannah! Hannah! Hannah!" That's the sound of thousands of Miley Cyrus/Hannah Montana fans screaming her name at the beginning of one of her concerts. And that sound is music to Cyrus's ears. She loves hearing the crowd shouting her name. She knows how important it is to have their support. The recognition she gets for her hard work is what makes it all worthwhile.

In addition to the recognition Cyrus gets from her fans, she has received her share of formal recognition too. And that tastes just as sweet.

Remember, Cyrus really only entered the spotlight in 2006. That is when the first episodes of *Hannah Montana* aired. It didn't take long for her to become a household name, though. The first year *Hannah Montana* was on, it became an instant success. It started with the highest ratings any Disney show had ever received. Fans went crazy.

Cyrus became an overnight sensation. In 2006, she was nominated for her first Teen Choice Award. The nomination was for Female TV Choice Breakout Star for her role on *Hannah Montana*. Even though she didn't win the award, it was a great honor to be nominated. The same year, Miley appeared on her first magazine cover. It was *Popstar!* magazine. Of course, if you go to a bookstore today, you might see her face on the cover of up to a half dozen magazines.

Over the next year, things just kept getting better. *Hannah Montana* became the number one cable TV show among viewers aged six to fourteen. The year 2007 was fantastic for Cyrus. The successful, funny starlet earned a number of awards and titles. She won the Teen Choice Award for Choice TV Actress in a Comedy for *Hannah Montana*. She also won the Teen Choice Award for Choice Summer Artist. Cyrus also won a Nickelodeon's Kids' Choice Award, and the Kids' Choice Award for Favorite TV Actress.

In 2007, Cyrus received the title "Poptastic Queen" from *Popstar!* magazine. She was named as one of *People* magazine's 100 Most Beautiful People in the World. She also came in at number seventeen on *Forbes* magazine's Top Twenty Earners Under 25. According to the magazine, Miley earned $3.5 million dollars in 2007.

▲ *Miley Cyrus blows a kiss to her fans at a fashion show.*

HANNAH STUFF

Being famous can be a lot of fun. Companies often give celebrities free products. They want the celebrity to use their products and to appear in their advertisements.

In 2004, Cyrus became the spokesperson for Daisy Rock Guitars. Daisy Rock makes guitars especially for female musicians. Cyrus and her dad were at a Country Music Television event when her parents gave her a Daisy guitar. They presented it to her in front of 30,000 people. It was Cyrus's favorite color—pink! This was before Miley was even well known. (Of course, her dad was already famous.)

Once the *Hannah Montana* craze started, all sorts of products related to the show started popping up. Among them is a set of *Hannah Montana* books. Each book includes photos and dialogue from an episode of the show. There are also *Hannah Montana* video games.

Cyrus is especially excited about the *Hannah Montana* clothing line. She says that the clothes are stylish and cute. She got to help design some of the pieces. They aren't too wild because they are for everyday wear. "It's not a costume," she explains. She says that girls wearing her clothes "want to look like they could be Hannah Montana's friend. This is a fashion line." On a trip back to Nashville, Cyrus tried on some of the *Hannah Montana* clothes in a store there. "This is weird. I'm wearing my face," she joked.

In addition to the *Hannah Montana* clothing line, Disney is making a bunch of other fun Hannah products. Fans will be

AWARDS

Fans aren't the only ones who think Miley Cyrus has talent. She's already won a number of awards for *Hannah Montana*!

2008
- Won a Gracie Allen Award for outstanding female lead in a comedy series
- Won a Kids' Choice Award for Favorite Television Actress
- Won a Young Artist Award for Best Performance in a TV Series by a Leading Young Actress
- Nominated for a Young Artist Award for Best Young Ensemble Performance in a TV series (shared with Emily Osment, Mitchel Musso, Moises Arias, and Cody Linley)

2007
- Won a Kids' Choice Award for Favorite Television Actress
- Won a Teen Choice Award for Choice TV Actress in a Comedy

2006
- Nominated for a Teen Choice Award for Choice TV Breakout Star

▲ *Miley Cyrus accepts her Teen Choice Award in 2007.*

41

able to buy stationery, greeting cards, posters, bed sheets, and even makeup and perfume.

Cyrus has her own official Web site, too, called *Miley World*. This is where fans can watch videos, play games, look at photos and videos of Cyrus, read the performer's diary, enter contests, and chat with other fans.

Cyrus wants to continue performing in the future. And she has both the drive and the confidence to make it happen. As the young star says, "If you believe in yourself, anything is possible." And she is living proof of that.

Miley Cyrus arrives at a party in 2007. Cyrus loves to be in ▶ the spotlight, and it looks like that's where she'll stay!

Timeline

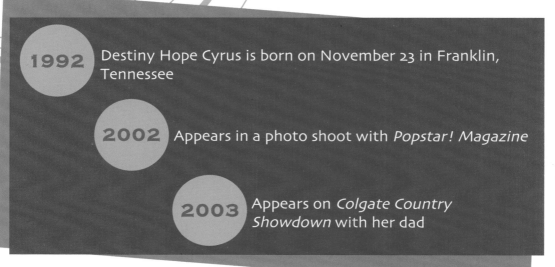

1992 Destiny Hope Cyrus is born on November 23 in Franklin, Tennessee

2002 Appears in a photo shoot with *Popstar! Magazine*

2003 Appears on *Colgate Country Showdown* with her dad

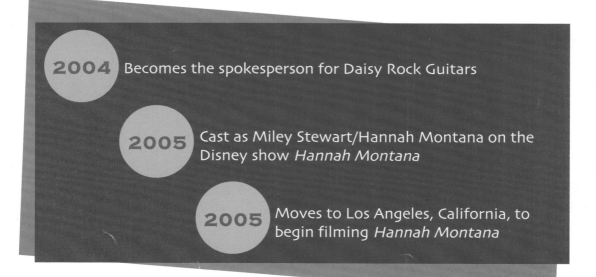

2004 Becomes the spokesperson for Daisy Rock Guitars

2005 Cast as Miley Stewart/Hannah Montana on the Disney show *Hannah Montana*

2005 Moves to Los Angeles, California, to begin filming *Hannah Montana*

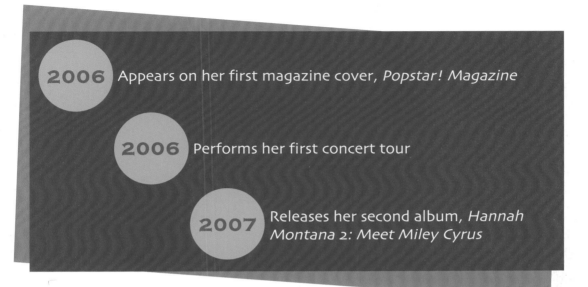

2006 Appears on her first magazine cover, *Popstar! Magazine*

2006 Performs her first concert tour

2007 Releases her second album, *Hannah Montana 2: Meet Miley Cyrus*

2007 Starts the North American *Best of Both Worlds* tour

2008 Legally changes her name from Destiny Hope Cyrus to Miley Ray Cyrus

2008 Releases first solo CD, *Breakout*

Further Info

BOOKS

Alexander, Lauren. *Mad for Miley: An Unauthorized Biography*. New York: Price Stearn Sloan, 2007.

Janic, Susan. *Living the Dream: Hannah Montana and Miley Cyrus, the Unofficial Story*. Toronto: ECW Press, 2008.

CDS AND DVDS

Cyrus, Miley. *Breakout*. Hollywood Records, 2008.

Hannah Montana: Life's What You Make It (2006). Walt Disney Home Entertainment, 2007.

INTERNET ADDRESSES

Miley Cyrus Official Site
http://www.mileycyrus.com/official

Miley World: The Miley Cyrus Official Fan Club
http://www.mileyworld.com/community/home

Glossary

audition—A short performance that tests an entertainer's abilities.

celebrity—A famous person, such as a television or movie star.

choreographer—Someone who arranges dance steps or movements for a show.

debuted—Appeared for the first time.

destiny—One's fate or the future events in one's life.

duet—A piece of music that is played or a song that is sung by two people.

lyrics—The words of a song.

nominated—Selected for the chance to win a prize, award, or election.

premiere—The first public performance of a movie or play.

recognition—Special notice or attention.

soundtrack—A recording of music from a movie or television show.

Index